ALSO AVAILABLE IN
# THE WISDOM OF SERIES

## ANCIENT GREECE
Compiled by Jacques Lacarrière
Photographs by Jacques Lacarrière

## ANCIENT ROME
Compiled by Benoît Desombres

## BUDDHA
Compiled by Marc de Smedt
Photographs by Jean-Louis Nou

## JESUS
Compiled by Jean-Yves Leloup

## JUDAISM
Compiled by Victor Malka
Illustrations by Marc Chagall

## TAO
Compiled by Marc de Smedt

## ZEN
Compiled by Marc de Smedt
Calligraphy by Master Taisen Deshimaru

*la ilaha illa allah*
*mohammadur rasoola allah*

# THE WISDOM OF
# ISLAM

### Compiled by Nacer Khémir

Illustrated with stills from two films by Nacer Khémir,
*Les Baliseurs du désert* and *Le Collier perdu de la colombe*

Abbeville Press   Publishers
New York   London   Paris

## To Sidi Muhammad El Khémir

Cover illustration and vignettes by Danielle Siegelbaum

For the English-language edition
RESEARCH, TRANSLATION FROM THE FRENCH, AND BIBLIOGRAPHY:
John O'Toole
EDITOR: Jacqueline Decter
TYPOGRAPHIC DESIGN: Virginia Pope
PRODUCTION EDITOR: Owen Dugan

For the original edition
SERIES EDITORS: Marc de Smedt and Michel Piquemal

First edition
10  9  8  7  6  5  4  3  2  1

Library of Congress Cataloging-in-Publication Data

Paroles d'Islam. English.
The wisdom of Islam/compiled by Nacer Khémir.
p.  cm.
Includes bibliographical references.
ISBN 0-7892-0237-9
1. Sufism—Prayer-books and devotions—English. I. Khémir,
Nacer. II. Title.
BP189.62.P3713  1996
297'.43—dc20                                          96–21419

From the seventh century A.D. on, Islam—and its corner-stone, the Koran—has played a part in forging the world's soul. Since the Prophet's revelation in Mecca and his exile to Medina, Muslims on four continents have brought about a true transformation of humanity and society. Islam has thus become one of the elements that make up our mental and historical universe.

From Arabia to India, Indonesia, Russia, and China, the Islamic faith has tried to reconcile religion, ideology, and history by always and everywhere placing the Koran at the heart of thought. As such Islam has taken shape in the difficult interplay of history and men, reflection and imagination. In the process it has given birth to a civilization. And although this Islamic culture is built up around divine revelation and a founding book, it promotes a way of life as much as a form of belief.

It is our duty then to lift Islam out of the rut of received wisdom and Islamist caricatures that reduce it to a series of certitudes, dogmas, and religious practices, and focus our attention rather on its humanity.

This humanity was already present in the personal path taken up by the founder of Islam, Mohammed, who shrank at times from both the revelation made to him and the role some wanted to see him play.

Far from the simplistic image of the triumphant warrior, two beings coexist within the Prophet, as within his fellow men and women. There is a human being, with his hesitations and weaknesses, and a being called to an eternal destiny. It is Islam's vocation to reassure man and help him surmount his weaknesses.

Between divine will and human limits lies a space that allows of human freedom. In this space man can create his own relationship with God, a relationship that needs no intermediary. And the very first thing he must do in paying homage to his Creator is to put his reason to use, that absolute gift made by God to his creature.

It is with heartfelt joy that Muslims give thanks to God for this privilege by exercising their reason here on earth, sharing it with others, and transmitting their knowledge to their fellow beings in order to remain faithful to the divine message.

The same holds for Nature, which Muslims "return" to the Creator after reworking, transforming, and occasionally "uplifting" it, as in those gardens that are meant to give us a foretaste of paradise here on earth. There is in this a magnificent way of embracing life, a capacity for happiness, and a sensuality that can be seen in gardens just as much as in certain homes and their interiors (jewelry, fabrics, rugs), in music, poetry, and stories.

The most sumptuous example of this is found in *The Thousand and One Nights*. Throughout its many pages this book suggests models for the good life and a refined code of social conduct through which a true ethics of happiness takes shape.

We are a far cry then from orthodox Islam, which rejects this direct relationship of an individual with God if it does not fall under collective law. Theologians staunchly committed to orthodoxy were to condemn the greatest mystics, including al-Hallaj, Suhrawardi, and Ibn Arabi, whose religious impulse is solitary. Such men and women were especially suspect since to express the flame of their belief, they borrowed from the language of *khamrya* (bacchanalian poetry) and *ghazal* (love poetry), diverting it from its profane meaning to attain the sacred.

Orthodox belief did everything in its power to exclude these mystics, going so far as to condemn some to the stake, as was the case with al-Hallaj, whose words thus resound even more intensely: *Kill me then, my faithful comrades, / In my murder lies my life.*

These theologians' terrible fear of the depth of this mystic love only brings to light the tepidness of their faith and the weakness of their spirituality.

How can one compare their dependence on a system of punishments and rewards with the fervor of a love like that expressed by the woman mystic Rabi'a al-Adawiyya, who raced through the streets of Baghdad carrying fire in one hand and water in the other, crying: *With these things I am going to set fire to Heaven / And put out the flames of Hell / So that voyagers to God can rip the veils / And see the real goal.*

Who are the madmen and who are the sages here? And what if they were none other than the "white thread" and the "black thread" that the Koran speaks of, its way of saying that only the dawn will enable us to distinguish one from the other?

If only the few words of Islamic wisdom mentioned in this volume—drawn from the Koran, as well as from various poems dedicated to love, God, and men—could lift for a moment the dark veil that some have thrown over this culture, perhaps then we might glimpse the Islam dear to the heart of the contemporary poet Jamal Eddin Bencheikh:

"The Islam that I claim as my own is faith not power, ethics not politics.

"I assert its spirituality against the hegemonic ambitions of a handful of its adepts.

"I put my faith in the harrowing passion of the prophet from Mecca, in the purity of his dream of eternity, not his autocratic conception of the state and hierarchic conception of society.

"His is not of my century and no one, as far as I know, can claim the right to come and interpret God for me.

"Islam gives me the signal privilege of being solely accountable for my acts."

Nacer Khémir

You created night, I made the lamp. You created clay, I made the cup. You created the forest, the mountain, and the desert; I made the walk, the garden, the orchard.

Mohammed Iqbal
Indian Muslim poet
(1875–1938)

Having drunk entire seas, we remain quite surprised that our lips are just as dry as the shore, and we continue to seek out the sea to dip them there, without seeing that our lips are the shore and we ourselves the sea.

Farid al-Din Attar
Persian mystic poet (died c. 1230)
*Manteq at-Tair* (*Conference of Birds*)

## The Blind Man

Once upon a time a dervish Shaykh saw a Koran in the house of a blind old man. He became his guest in the month of Tamuz.... He said to himself, "Oh, I wonder what the Book is here for, as this righteous dervish is blind.... No one lives here except him.... But I am not so unmannerly or muddled as to ask him the reason. Nay, hush! I will be patient, in order that by patience I may gain my object...."

At midnight he heard the sound of recitation of the Koran; he sprang up from sleep and beheld a marvel: The blind man was reading correctly from the Koran....

"Oh, wonderful!" he cried. "You with sightless eyes, how are you reading, how are you seeing the lines?"

He replied, "I begged of God, crying, 'O You whose help is sought, I am as covetous of reading the Book as I am of life. I do not know it by heart: at the time of reading it, bestow on my two eyes an untroubled light....'

"That incomparable King at once gives my sight back to me, like a lamp that makes an end of night."

Jalal al-Din Rumi
Sufi mystic poet (1207–1273),
founder of the order of dervishes
*The Mathnawi*

One day a novice came to beg instruction of a Sufi master.

"First you must find the answer to one question," a disciple said to him. "If you are able to, the master will accept you as a student in three years."

The student was asked the question and spared no effort until he found the solution. The Sufi's disciple conveyed the answer to the master and returned with this message:

"Your answer is correct. You may go and wait until one thousand and one days have passed; then you may come back for Instruction."

The novice was overjoyed. He thanked the messenger and asked him: "And what would have happened had I not given the right answer?"

"Oh, in that case you would have been admitted immediately!"

Sufi tale

Know that the whole world is a mirror, in each atom are found a hundred blazing suns. If you split the center of a single drop of water, a hundred pure oceans spring forth. If you examine each particle of dust, a thousand Adams can be seen....

A universe lies hidden in a grain of millet; everything is brought together at the point of the present…. From each point along that circle thousands of forms are drawn. Each point, as it revolves in a circle, is at times a circle, at others a turning circumference.

Mahmud Shabestari
Sufi poet from Iran
(fourteenth century)

God has hidden the sea and revealed the foam, he has hidden the wind and revealed the dust.... How could the dust rise of itself.... Yet you see the dust, not the wind. How could the foam move without the sea? But you see the foam and not the sea.

Jalal al-Din Rumi
Sufi mystic poet (1207–1273)

*The Ant in Love*

Walking one day in a lonely place King Solomon chanced upon an ant hill. All the ants immediately came out by the thousands to hail the king. Only one of their number took no notice of him, for it was busy carrying off grain by grain the enormous pile of sand rising before it. King Solomon called the insect before him and said:

"O tiny ant, even with the longevity of Noah and the patience of Job, you will never make this mountain of sand disappear!"

"O great King," said the ant, "Do not regard my size alone…but take heed of my ardor as well. Behind this mound stands my beloved. Nothing shall stop me from leveling it. And if I must lose my life, at least I shall die in the hope of reaching her."

O King, learn from an ant what the power of love is, learn from a blind man the secret of vision.

Farid al-Din Attar
Persian mystic poet
(died c. 1230)

Someone once asked me how old I was, having seen my advanced age turning to gray at my temples and in the locks along my forehead.

I answered, "One hour. For verily, I count the time I have lived as nothing."

He replied, "What do you mean? Explain. Here is indeed the most moving of things."

I said: "One day, by surprise, I stole a kiss, a secret kiss, from her who has my heart. However many my days may number, I shall count only that brief moment, for it was truly my entire life."

Ibn Hazm
Andalusian writer (994–1064)
*Tawq al-Hamama* (*The Dove's Neck Ring*)

One cannot contemplate God directly without any medium (either perceptible or spiritual), for God per se is independent of any one world.... The Contemplation of God in women is the most intense and the most perfect; and the most intense union (within the perceptible order that serves as a medium for such contemplation) is the act of love.

Ibn Arabi
Andalusian mystic poet
(1165–1240)

One day Rabi'a* was asked how she saw love:

"Between the lover and the beloved," she replied, "there is no distance. There are words only through the power of desire, description only through Taste. He who has tasted has come to know, and he who has described has not described himself. In truth, how can you describe something when, in its presence, you are absent, in its existence, you are dissolved, in its contemplation, you are undone, in its purity, you are intoxicated, in your surrender, you are fulfilled, in your joy, you are parted from yourself?"

*Rabi'a al-Adawiyya (717?–801)
Muslim woman mystic from Basra

*The Lover*

A man madly in love knocked on the door of his beloved. She asked from behind the door: "Who is there?" He answered: "It is I!" And she replied: "There is not enough room for both you and me in the same house." So he betook himself to the desert to meditate. Years later he came back and knocked on her door. The voice of his beloved asked: "Who is it?" He answered: "It is you yourself!" And the door opened wide.

After Ibn Arabi
Andalusian mystic poet
(1165–1240)

One day while Majnun* was sighing deeply for his beloved, someone came and said to him: "Majnun, leave off with your laments for Laila is coming to see you. Even now she is at your door." Majnun immediately raised his head: "Tell her to go away, for Laila would prevent me for a moment from thinking of my love for Laila."

From *Al Aghani* (*The Book of Songs*)

*Seventh-century poet who died for his love of Laila

*The Prophet said:*

*Die before dying.*

"I fear death," said the birds.

"Can death exist for one whose heart is joined with God?" replied the hoopoe. "My heart is one with Him, thus time and death no longer exist for me. For death is the suspension of time, and time is born of our attachment to things that perish."

Farid al-Din Attar
Persian mystic poet (died c. 1230)
*Manteq at-Tair* (*Conference of Birds*)

Never had I bemoaned adversity; never had I felt troubled before the numerous cares that assailed me…until the day I found myself shoeless and without a penny to buy a pair of babouches. Dejected, I entered the mosque of Kufa in order to unburden my heavy heart with prayer. And there I saw a man who had no feet. I therefore thanked God and patiently bore my lack of slippers.

Mucharrif al-Din Sa'di
Sufi mystic poet, Baghdad (c. 1184–c. 1291)
*Gulistan* (*The Rose Garden*)

*Rich and Poor*

Famine gripped the land. Yet for all that not everyone was dying of hunger: the rich had taken care to set aside ample stores of wheat, oil, dried vegetables and meats. So Khadija said to her husband: "Nasr Eddin, the whole town considers you a wise man. Do not sit there with your arms crossed, doing nothing; go to the square, call the people together, and try to convince the rich to give the poor something to eat." For once Nasr Eddin found that his wife was right. He did as she said, and two hours later returned home, his face radiant.

"My wife, let us give thanks to Allah the Merciful!"
"Ah, so you have succeeded?"
"It was no easy mission. Only partly."
"What do you mean partly?"
"Exactly: I have succeeded in convincing the poor."

Nasr Eddin Hodja
Traditional figure of comedy and wisdom
in Arabic, Turkish, and Persian tales

## On Pure Love

God said to one of His servants, "Do you claim to love Me? If so, know that your love for Me is only the result of My love for you. You love Him who is. I loved you while you were not!"

He then said to him, "Do you claim to seek to draw near Me, and to lose yourself in Me? Yet I seek you far more than you seek Me! I sought you so that you would be in My presence, without any intermediary, the Day I said, "Am I not your Lord?" [Koran, sura 7:172] while you were only spirit. Then you forgot Me, and I sought you once again, sending to you My emissaries when you had a body. All of that was love for you and not for Me."

Mawqif 112
Amir Abd al-Qadir (1807?–1883)
Mystic and hero in the struggle for Algerian independence

And if the Wine you drink, the Lip you press,
End in the Nothing all Things end in—Yes—
Then fancy while Thou art, Thou art but what
Thou shalt be—Nothing—Thou shalt not be less.

While the Rose blows along the River Brink,
With old Khayyam the Ruby Vintage drink:
And when the Angel with his darker Draught
Draws up to Thee—take that, and do not shrink.

Omar Khayyam
Sufi poet, c. 1047–c. 1122
*The Rubaiyat*, XLVII, XLVIII
(Edward Fitzgerald's translation)

## The Book of Spiritual Stayings
### Mawqif of "Who Art Thou And Who Am I"

He stayed me, and said to me: Who art thou, and who am I? And I saw the sun and the moon, the stars, and all the lights. And He said to me: There remains no light in the current of my sea which thou hast not seen. And everything came to me, until there remained naught: and each thing kissed me between the eyes, and greeted me, and stayed in the shadow. And He said to me: Thou knowest Me, but I do not know thee.

And I saw the whole of Him connected with my vesture, and not connected with Me. And He said: This is my service. And my vesture inclined, but I did not incline. And when my vesture inclined, He said to me: Who am I? And the sun and the moon were darkened, and the stars fell from the sky, and the lights grew pale, and darkness covered everything save Him. And everything spoke, and said: God is most great. And everything came to me, bearing in its hand a lance. And He said to me: Flee. And I said: Whither shall I flee? And He said: Fall into the darkness. And I fell into the darkness, and beheld myself. And He said: Thou shalt never more behold other than thyself, and thou shalt not go forth from the darkness henceforth forever: but when I expel thee from it, I shall show thee Myself, and thou shalt see Me; and when thou seest Me, yet shalt thou be further from Me than all that are far.

Muhammad ibn Abd al-Jabbar al-Niffari
Mystic from Kufa in Irak (died 965)

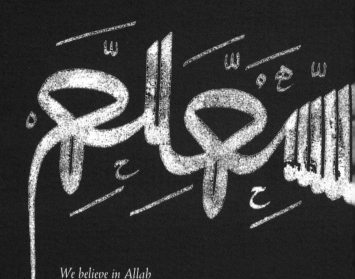

*We believe in Allah*

*and that which is revealed unto us,*

*and that which was revealed unto Abraham,*

*and Ishmael, and Isaac, and Jacob, and the tribes,*

*and that which Moses and Jesus received,*

*and that which the prophets received from their Lord.*

*We make no distinction between any of them.*

The Koran, sura 2:136

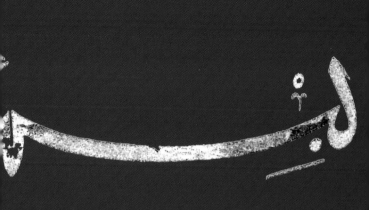

*Do you not see how Allah is praised*

*by those in heaven and earth?*

*The very birds praise Him*

*as they wing their flight.*

The Koran, sura 24:41

My heart

Has become capable

Of taking all sorts of forms;

It is

Pastures

For gazelles

And

Monastery for the monk,

Temple for idols

And

Kaaba for the pilgrim.

It is the tables of the Torah

And

The Book of the Koran.

It professes the religion of love

Whatever the place

Toward which

Its caravans wend.

And love

Is

My law

And love

Is

My faith.

Ibn Arabi
Mystic Islamic poet
(1165–1240)

*Your image is in my eye*

*Your invocation is on my lips*

*Your abode is in my heart*

*Where then can You be absent?*

Husayn ibn Mansur al-Hallaj
Mystic Islamic poet
(Baghdad 858/9–922)

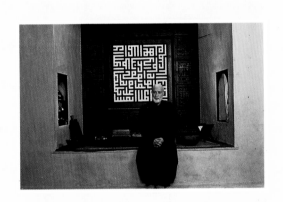

Born in Tunisia, Nacer Khémir is both a filmmaker and a storyteller. Since 1978 he has performed in more than a thousand towns and villages. In 1982, and again in 1988, he recounted the *Thousand and One Nights* each evening for a month at the Théâtre National de Chaillot in Paris.

In addition, Mr. Khémir has published several collections of tales in French.

As for the cinema, he shot his first feature-length film, entitled *Histoires du Pays du Bon Dieu*, in 1976. In 1985 he directed a feature-length color film, *Les Baliseurs du désert*, which won the Grand Prix at the Valence Film Festival and several other awards.

His latest film, *Le Collier perdu de la colombe*, completed in 1990, received the jury's Prix Spécial at the Locarno Film Festival and a number of other awards.

The photographs illustrating this volume are stills from *Le Baliseurs* and *Le Collier perdu*. Those on the endpapers and pages 6, 11, 24, and 26 were shot during the filming of *Le Collier perdu* by G.M. Zimmermann © SYGMA.

# Selected Bibliography

The founding text of Islam, the Koran, has been translated into English a number of times. Penguin, for instance, offers a paperback edition of N. J. Dawood's translation (1956). A. J. Arberry's translation is also available in a paperback edition (Collier Books, 1955). Marmaduke Pickthall's translation has been reissued by Everyman's Library (1992). For bilingual editions, readers may wish to consult Pickthall's translation in the Fine Books edition (1976), or Abdullah Yusuf Ali's version (with extensive notes) published by the Islamic Center (1978).

Arberry, A. J. *Jalal al-Din Rumi: Selections*. Chicago: University of Chicago Press, 1991.

Nicholson, Reynold A. *The Mathnawí of Jalalu'ddín Rúmí*. Cambridge: Cambridge University Press, 1930. (This classic text in prose and verse contains a great number of highly enjoyable tales interspersed throughout its many pages. See the following for an anthology of such tales drawn from Nicholson's great translation.)

————. *Tales of Mystic Meaning: Selections from the Mathnawí*. Oxford: Oneworld, 1995.

Peters, F. E. *A Reader on Classical Islam*. Princeton: Princeton University Press, 1994.

Salahi, M. A. *Muhammad, Man and Prophet: A Complete Study of the Life of the Prophet of Islam*. Shaftesbury, Dorset, England: Element, 1995.

Smith, Margaret. *Rabia: The Life and Work of Rabia and Other Women Mystics in Islam*. Oxford: Oneworld, 1994.

————. *Studies in Early Mysticism in the Near and Middle East*. Oxford: Oneworld, 1995.

Upton, Charles. *Doorkeeper of the Heart: Versions of Rabi'a*. Brattleboro, Vt.: Threshold Books, 1988.

Waines, David. *An Introduction to Islam*. Cambridge, England: Cambridge University Press, 1995.

Zakaria, Rafiq. *Muhammad and the Quran*. London: Penguin, 1991.